D1046778

Weekly Reader Children's Book Club presents

Moon-Watch Summer

WEEKLY READER
CHILDREN'S BOOK CLUB
This is a registered trademark

also by Lenore and Erik Blegvad

Mr. Jensen and Cat
One Is for the Sun
The Great Hamster Hunt

Moon-Watch Summer

Lenore Blegvad

With illustrations by
Erik Blegvad

New York
Harcourt Brace Jovanovich, Inc.

DISCARD

36862

J
BLE

2/3/4 *gift Jamie Ware Laz*

Text copyright © 1972 by Lenore Blegvad
Illustrations copyright © 1972 by Erik Blegvad
All rights reserved. No part of this publication may be reproduced
or transmitted in any form or by any means, electronic or mechanical,
including photocopy, recording, or any information storage and
retrieval system, without permission in writing from the publisher.
Library of Congress Catalog Card Number: 74-187855
ISBN 0-15-255350-9
Printed in the United States of America

Weekly Reader Children's Book Club Edition

Moon-Watch Summer

Wednesday afternoon

"Has she got television?" Adam asked. "Otherwise, I'm not going."

"You're going anyway," his father told him. "Grammie is all alone this summer. You and Jenny will keep her company, and we will come when we can."

"OK," Adam said, "OK. But *has* she got TV up on that farm or not?"

"Perhaps," his mother said. She was busy packing suitcases. "I honestly can't remember. It's too bad that Dad and I have to make this trip now, of all times, but that's just the way it is."

"That's the way it always is," Adam said to himself. Another sudden business trip, this one all the way across the Atlantic. "Now, of all times" was right! He was horrified. It was the summer of the first moon landing, and there was absolutely nothing on his mind except the moon.

That very morning the whole family had watched the televised beginning of another journey—one that Adam had waited a long, long time to see: the roaring, fiery blast-off of the Apollo 11 spacecraft, on its way to land the first men on the moon.

It was now five hours into the mission. Out in space the Apollo 11 crew were relaxing. They had performed the first complicated maneuvers of the flight to perfection. Adam had followed them through each step as it was announced by teams of television experts. He would have liked to relax for a while himself. But he could think of nothing except that tomorrow he had to leave for Grammie's farm, where there was perhaps no television at all. Could it really be happening to him? Impossible!

Thursday morning

Traveling to Grammie's in the train the next day, four-year-old Jenny bounced on the plush seat opposite Adam. She watched everything outside the window with the greatest interest: first, the tall city buildings, the river, and the stations, then the increasing greenery, the country houses, the gardens, all flashing by the window and spreading out behind them.

During the tunnels she stared at her own reflection in the glass, at her straggly bangs and dark eyes. Or,

turning her head one way and the other, she compared
her brother to his reflected image. Was his hair as dark
as it looked in the window? No, it was lighter, but just
as straight. Did he really look as grumpy as that? Yes,
he really did.

Adam did not look out of the window, and he barely
spoke. It was a long ride. He remembered taking the
same trip once before, seven years ago, but not without

his parents as he and Jenny were doing now. Since he was eleven now, he must have been just about Jenny's age then. The next year he and his parents had moved out to the West where Jenny was born. And now, unexpectedly as usual, they had just moved back again to the East. Jenny had never met Grammie. But she acted as if she knew her better than Adam did, writing her letters and sending her scribbly crayon drawings all the time.

Another train rushed past in the opposite direction. Adam wished he were on it. He glanced at the luggage rack overhead. His charts were still all right. He had rolled them up carefully and tied them with a string. There was a chart of the moon itself, and one of the spacecraft, another of the probable landing site, and timetables of each maneuver. He had made them himself, during the past few weeks.

Adam looked at his watch. It was twenty-eight hours into the mission—time, he knew, for the astronauts to eat their lunch: frankfurters, applesauce, and chocolate pudding squeezed from tubes.

Adam and Jenny, feeling hungry as well, ate the tuna-fish sandwiches their mother had packed for them.

Thursday afternoon

Grammie was at the tiny station, come to fetch them in a hired taxi. She didn't even have a car! Adam kissed her only briefly and scowled at her behind her back. But she didn't notice. She was busy making friends with Jenny. Adam thought she hadn't changed much since the first time he had seen her. Or perhaps he didn't notice it. Her hair had been gray then as well, and sort of free blowing, and she had dressed then, as now, in what he would have called "pioneer clothes," hard-wearing and simple.

The taxi drove out of town along the river; the winding road hugged close to the rock-strewn riverbed. Trees beside the road cast long late-afternoon shadows.

Jenny took a quick look at Adam. Then he heard her ask, "Grammie, have you got a television?"

The taxi rumbled across a wooden bridge. Grammie said she was sorry. She did not have television. "But there are so many other things to do. You'll see."

Adam did not show he had heard. Stony-faced, he stared into the pine forests as the car, crossing another wooden bridge, began the slow climb up the dirt road to Grammie's house.

And elsewhere the three astronauts were climbing

as well, climbing through space toward the moon, at 4,486 feet per second.

"This is your old room, Adam. Do you remember it?" Up under the eaves, it had a sloping wall. A dormer window was framed by white curtains, which moved in the breeze from the valley below. Beyond the window the valley itself rushed down in steps of meadow and woods and climbed up again on the opposite slopes.

"What's that on the top?" Adam asked, pointing to the highest part of the facing mountain. Grammie looked.

"That? That's the new ski lift. They've almost finished building it. And, I might add, all the ski huts and beer halls and hot-dog stands that go along with it." She turned her back to the window.

One of Grammie's many cats was curled up on Adam's bed, denting the quilt. He did not remember the cat, although Grammie said it had been here when he had been, many summers before. But the view out of the little window into the rapidly dropping valley seemed rather like something he had dreamed long, long ago.

They unpacked their things and went out to see the garden. It tilted along the top edge of the meadow below the house. "Now what do you think this is?" asked Grammie. A row of pale fernlike greenery lay before their feet. They did not know what it was. "Pull one up," Grammie invited Adam.

He did not move. So Jenny knelt and gave a tug. A

carrot slid smoothly from the soil. Jenny was delighted. "Carrots!"

Grammie pointed to the next row. "And this?" Jenny pulled again. Radishes! There were tomato plants staked and tied with bits of rag, beans swinging from their vines, cornstalks not yet fully grown, rows of lettuces. Jenny touched them all, greeting them like old friends she had never expected to see in such a strange new place. Adam paid no attention. He looked down the hillside to where the trees began again at the bottom.

"What's down there?" he asked.

"The brook. Don't you remember? Grandpa used to take you to build dams and sail leaf boats in the pools."

He wasn't sure. It was such a long time ago.

"Isn't there a house there?"

Grammie nodded. "That's right. It used to be a nice little farmhouse when you were here. But it's been bought by the people who are building the ski lift. It's a very modern place now!"

Adam searched the trees. He could see no sign of the house through them. "Do you think they have television?"

Grammie laughed. "I wouldn't be surprised if they have one in every room." She and Jenny picked some tomatoes and a head of lettuce. Jenny said good night

to a row of radishes she had already become fond of, and they went in to prepare supper.

Adam followed them slowly. He would go down there tomorrow, to the house by the brook. From the porch he turned and looked into the valley. He still couldn't see the house—just the vast sweep of green meadows and trees down and up the other side. Nothing.

And out in space the astronauts gazed down in fascination at the earth. They were just about halfway between it and the moon.

Thursday evening

"Sit next to me," Jenny said, tugging at Adam when it was time to eat. They had helped to set the table in the big kitchen, where Jenny's crayon drawings were very much to be seen, tacked on almost every wall. Pots of plants stood on the windowsills, and on each chair around the table lay one of Grammie's cats. Grammie shooed them away. Jenny was sorry for them.

"Don't be," Grammie told her. "They have eaten, and now it's our turn. They'll just have to take their naps somewhere else."

Jenny inched her chair closer to Adam's. He frowned at her.

"When are Mommy and Daddy coming, Adam?" she asked him in a small voice.

Adam shrugged. *"I* don't know," he said. "We only just got here *ourselves."*

Grammie set a platter of chops and peas and browned potatoes by Jenny's place. "They'll be coming as soon as they can. Perhaps in two or three weeks," she said soothingly. "But for tonight, why don't you be the mother, Jenny? How would you like to serve the dinner?"

Jenny was pleased. She grasped the big serving spoon and divided everything into equal portions. Adam watched her impatiently. "Oh, for crying out loud!" he said when she even began to count out the green peas. But when they had eaten, they both felt better. The salad from the garden was so fresh and green that Adam thought it was the best part of the meal. But he didn't say so. At that very moment, when Apollo 11 was due to send a lengthy color TV transmission to earth which he would not see, Adam did not feel like talking about the food or, indeed, about anything at all.

Grammie's house was almost two hundred years old. It had been built just after the Revolution, in 1781. When Grammie and Grandpa had bought the farm, before Adam was born, they had learned to farm the land around it. Once there had been two farm workers to help. And once there had been cows and several horses. Now Grammie did not farm the land except for her vegetable garden. There was only one old swaybacked horse left, a brown soft-nosed horse called Lisa, who stood tethered in a sloping pasture up behind the house. The house itself still had its old wide floorboards, stained to a dark brown. Heavy beams crossed the ceilings in every room. Those in the living room bristled with iron hooks that once had been used to hang meat. There was also an enormous fireplace, made of stones dug from the rocky meadows.

Hanging on the living-room wall was a photograph of Adam that showed him standing inside the rocky opening of the fireplace. His grandfather had taken it the summer Adam had been there. There were other photographs as well. Some of them they had copies of at home. Most of them showed Grandpa doing things around the farm. He had died last year without ever having met Jenny. There were pictures of him digging in his garden, admiring his views, and, best of all, one showing just his legs sticking out of a haystack into which he had pretended to fall.

He had been a heavy man, with thick untidy hair and a suggestion of a smile always present. Could Adam remember him? Adam no longer knew. He had seen so many photos and it was so long ago.

"Tell me about Grandpa," Jenny had said in the train. "I can't," Adam had replied. "I've forgotten him."

"Is that a radio?" Adam asked Grammie after supper. He couldn't tell for sure. It came from an age when radios looked like other things. This one was made of brown wood and shaped like the pointy window of a church. Grammie said it was, however, just that: a radio. She was curled up in a big chair reading to Jenny, who had found some storybooks.

"Does it work?" Adam asked, knowing it wouldn't.

"It should," said Grammie. "It was all right yesterday."

Yesterday? Adam was amazed. Grammie listened to the radio, up here on the mountaintop? What did she listen to? Probably gardening programs and weather reports. Farmers always listened to weather reports. But then, so did the Space Center. That gave Grammie and the Space Center something in common. Adam almost laughed out loud. Grammie looked up at him.

"What about that big roll of pictures you brought with you, Adam? Why not put them up on your wall? There's some tape on the desk in your room that you

can use. And you can borrow the radio, too, if you like."

Could he? He had been hoping not to have to listen to baby stories for Jenny. But his mother had told him, "Don't disappear all the time. You're there to keep Grammie company, remember."

Now in his room, with Grammie's old radio, he could make contact again with his own world. He plugged it into the wall outlet he found behind his desk, and after fiddling with the dials, he soon had what he wanted. A strong voice coming to him over the mountains and meadows told him that the space flight was proceeding normally. The astronauts were in excellent condition. During the television transmission Adam had just missed, they had described how to make chicken stew on the way to the moon and demonstrated the effect of weightlessness by setting a flashlight loose in the cabin. Adam marked it all down carefully on his charts. Then, from his window, he searched the sky for some glimpse of the moon. The sun had just set behind the now black mountain opposite, but the weather reports had been correct. Clouds were beginning to form, and through them nothing of the new moon in its first quarter could be seen.

Grammie brought Jenny upstairs to put her to bed. When she was ready, Jenny came into Adam's room in her nightgown. In one arm she held her bedraggled panda bear. "Will you come and say good night to Panda and me?" she asked.

Panda looked funny there in the farmhouse instead of in their apartment in the city.

"Yeah, OK," Adam agreed. "When you get in bed." But he felt silly. She wanted a good-night kiss, and he gave her one. But who did she think he was, her daddy or something?

Grammie was waiting in the hall. By chance, through the open door of Adam's room, she spied his moon map on the wall. Her face lit up. "Ah," she said. "The moon. The Sea of Rainbows. I've always been in love with the Sea of Rainbows. Perhaps it's the name."

Adam stared at her. She smiled and gave him a kiss on the cheek. "You don't mind if I go to bed as early as Jenny tonight? It's all that driving up and down the mountain in taxis. You'll manage all right? There are towels in the bathroom, and you can leave the hall light on when you go to bed."

Adam stared at her. "Yes, thank you, Grammie. Good night." Grammie closed her door.

The Sea of Rainbows! Grammie was in love with the Sea of Rainbows! What do you know about that?

Sometime later Adam turned off his radio, and the farmhouse was quiet. Outside in the sloping fields crickets chirped. He could hear frogs calling from the damp grasses along the edge of the brook below. With the touch of cool air from the pine woods on his face, Adam lay under his quilt and thought about the astronauts. Enclosed in their capsule, they were also at rest for the night, moving farther and farther away from him at every moment.

Friday morning

Adam was up early. Downstairs, he found Grammie, already drinking her morning tea. The cats, drinking milk, were spaced like the spokes of a wheel around their bowl. Sunshine sparkled through the flower vases. There was the smell of baking. The only noise was the lapping of cats and the deep tick of a clock.

"Do you want breakfast now," Grammie asked, "or do you want to wait for Jenny? She's still sleeping."

He said he would wait for Jenny. He wanted to get outside, to be by himself. It had been a shock to wake up and find himself at Grammie's that morning.

"I'll go out and look around," Adam said, heading for the door.

"You can walk down to the mailbox," Grammie suggested. "The paper will be there soon. I know you'll want some news about the moon shot. And here's something to nibble on along the way." It was a fresh-baked muffin, and taking it, Adam managed a half smile of thanks.

Outside, he stopped on the porch. The whole valley below lay bathed in early morning sun. It really looked good. Adam took a bite of his muffin and found it was filled with warm melting butter. He felt a sudden daze of pleasure. Finishing the muffin down to the last crumb, he licked his buttery fingers carefully before he started down the steps. But for a moment he had almost forgotten where he was going, and why.

Over Adam's head the sky was pale and transparent. As he walked, he stared into it where it touched the opposite hills. He sensed its cloudless depth stretching all the way from him to Cape Kennedy and outward, outward as far as the moon. It reminded him of the first time he had ever swum in the ocean. He had walked carefully into the water, touching with his toes the same waves that had washed other continents.

When he reached the mailbox, it was empty. He was too early. Well, of course, a useless little country paper wouldn't be delivered on time, anyway. He'd be lucky if there was anything in it about the moon shot at all. Oh, why was he here now, of all times, surrounded by meadows and mountains and small-town newspapers! He looked unhappily up and down the steep, wooded slopes. Below him, quite far down, he saw a glimpse of white. The little house by the brook! Adam began to run, his sneakers scattering pebbles as he went.

When he reached the brook, he stood for a while on the wooden bridge. The water, rippling downstream over boulders, came gurgling beneath the boards. Hearing it, he almost remembered having heard it before. And farther upstream had he once waded in shallow pools, sailing boats made out of twigs and leaves? On the other side of the bridge the brook formed a big pool, which Adam felt very sure he had never seen before. By its edge stood a modern house with a big picture window. Was that the little farmhouse he remembered? How everything had changed!

In the driveway to the modern house stood a shiny car with its engine running. There was no one in sight. But looking up, Adam saw what he had come for. There was an enormous television aerial on the roof! Did they have TV in every room as Grammie had said? Well, one would be good enough for him.

The door of the house opened and two men came out. One slung himself into the driver's seat of the car. The other, larger one, walked around the car to the other side and opened the door. Before getting in, he settled his sunglasses on his rather thin nose. Testing them against the still early sunlight, he noticed Adam standing at the end of the drive and nodded at him in a friendly way. Suddenly Adam felt panicky. They were going away! He had to speak to them now!

He moved toward the car, calling, "Is this your

house, Mister?" in a rather high-pitched voice.

"Yes. You looking for me?" The man paused with his foot inside the car.

"Well, no, not . . . I mean . . . yes, I am," Adam began in great confusion. "I was going to ask if you . . . I . . . if you would let me come and watch the moon-walk on your TV. I mean, we don't have TV up at our house, and I'm trying to find some way to get to see it."

How silly it sounded! But they were leaving and he had to ask now, no matter what it sounded like. He had to know!

The man looked somewhat startled. "The moon-

walk? But isn't that going to be in the middle of the night, two in the morning or something?" Adam nodded. "Well, I don't know. It's a funny time to have strangers coming in to watch TV. Why don't you ask somebody else? Don't you know anybody else around here?"

The man inside the car said something. The other bent down to hear him. Then, turning again to Adam, he asked, "What's your name, sonny?"

Adam told him and explained that his grandmother lived in the farm just above them on the mountainside and that she had no TV.

The man, whose straight, pale eyebrows had risen above the top of his sunglasses at the mention of Adam's name, nodded understandingly. Then he put his head inside the car again, and Adam heard him repeat his story. And immediately, to Adam's great surprise, everything was all right! He was given a large smile and a pat on the shoulder and told he could certainly come to watch the moon-walk. He could, in fact, come anytime he liked. But he must promise to bring his grandmother, too, and anyone else in the family who cared to come. What was more, since his grandmother had no car, they would be fetched in this very one just before the moon-walk was scheduled and brought home again when it was over.

Adam was delighted! So were the men. He could hear it in their voices and see it in their cheerful waves as they drove off. Adam watched the car as it turned out of the driveway toward the road leading to the new ski lift. In the still morning air he could hear its progress far along the road.

Feeling very pleased with himself, Adam began the slow climb toward home. It was a good beginning to the day. All around him the pines thrust their green fingers into the boundless skies and shaded him in a gigantic airy, whispering room.

Far out in space, the astronauts, too, were beginning their day, their third in the crowded quarters of the spacecraft.

"Do you want to come with us, Adam? We're going up to the pasture to see Lisa."

Breakfast was over and Adam had just finished putting all the information from the morning newspaper on his space charts. The paper had been full of the space flight. He had been quite wrong about that.

"Yes," he said. "I'll come." It might be a good time to tell Grammie about his visit to the house by the brook. He hadn't been able to at breakfast at all.

Jenny ran ahead of them, up through the sloping meadow. Last of the three, Adam pushed slowly through the long grass. It lay crushed in wide rivers behind him. There was the sound of katydids all around. Once a grasshopper jumped up inside the leg of his jeans, and he had to stop to shake it out. The ground felt bumpy underneath the thick grass. Soon they came to a stone wall with a wide wooden gate. Grammie opened the latch, and they slipped through into Lisa's pasture. There the grass was cropped tight and short and followed the bumps in the ground like green fur. Old Lisa lifted her head when they appeared. Grammie whistled to her, and she came ambling slowly over to them, her swaybacked shape looming enormously beside Jenny.

"Why is her back like that?" Jenny asked, reaching up to touch Lisa's graying velvet nose.

"She's very old, that's why," Grammie answered in a voice that was sad.

Carefully Adam stroked Lisa's muzzle. Had it taken Jenny to show him how not to be afraid? He realized he had never felt anything so deliciously smooth and warm. He looked into Lisa's great dark eye, rimmed with long lashes, and thought he had never seen a gentler look.

"Hold me up," Jenny said. Adam obligingly lifted her a foot or two off the ground. Leaning forward, she kissed Lisa on the nose.

"I love you, Lisa," Jenny told the horse, who softly stamped one hoof. Adam put Jenny down.

"How can you love a horse, stupid?" he said impatiently. Grammie stroked Lisa's long neck. She had brought some crackers and pieces of apple with her, and they were taking turns feeding Lisa from flat open palms.

"If the horse is Lisa, it's easy," Grammie said. Maybe, Adam thought, but it sure sounded silly to say so.

Friday afternoon

Jenny was having a long nap, and Grammie went out to work in the garden. Adam decided to help. He turned earth with a pitchfork and every now and then stopped to look into the valley, which was hazy with heat. The bright sky drew his thoughts again to the spacecraft. The latest radio reports had been good. Apollo 11 was on a perfect course.

Grammie seemed to read his thoughts. Peering at him from under her straw sun hat, she asked, "What news from space, Adam?"

He told her. Then he asked, "How come you're interested in the moon, Grammie?"

She laughed. "Isn't everybody?" There was a white butterfly circling around her hat. They both watched it as it fluttered uncertainly away into the valley. "I have always loved the moon," Grammie continued. "I'm really a sort of ancient moon-worshipper. I like all the superstitions and myths about it, the different stories of its origin from different parts of the world. I never look at the new moon over my left shoulder, of course. That brings bad luck, you know." She peeked at him under her hat brim. "And you mustn't point at it—that makes it angry. But it can be very helpful in planting, I've discovered. If you put seedlings in the earth at just the right time, they will grow wonderfully as the moon waxes. And then of course," Grammie continued enthusiastically, "there are all those lovely gods and goddesses associated with the moon: Diana, Varuna, Tsuki-Yomi. I can never decide which ones I like the best, the Roman or the Hindu or the Japanese. Perhaps the Greek. Or the Aztec. What about you, Adam. Which do you prefer?"

To all this, Adam gave a snort of impatience. "But I don't mean that stuff at all! That's not what I meant! I don't believe in any of that. I'm talking about the moon shot. What do you think about that?"

Grammie dug into the earth for a bit with her trowel. Then at last she said, "Well, I think it is certainly a great achievement and a great adventure."

"Is *that* all?" Adam gaped at her in astonishment. Then he began to chop sullenly at the ground with his pitchfork. "It's a lot more than that," he muttered. "A lot more. It's . . . it's the most important thing that ever happened; that's what it is!" he finished in a final burst.

Grammie took a little package of radish seeds from her gardening basket. She opened it carefully and poured a few of them into her hand. "Perhaps it's the

35

most fascinating," she said, peering down at them, "but I don't think it's the most important. At least, not to me. However, *I'm* very old-fashioned, you know."

Adam scowled. She sure was, he thought. "Well, what *is* more important?" he demanded. "What kind of thing?"

Grammie thought for a moment. Then she said, "The earth, I think. Just that. And the people on it. How they live and how they die. And the things that grow." She looked up at him again and smiled. "You'll be angry with me, I'm sure. But these little radish seeds are in a small way more important to me."

Radish seeds! Adam felt disgusted with everything. Well, what could you expect? He returned to his digging, turning over the heavy earth in great chunks. Suddenly he said, "I went down to that house—the one by the brook. I spoke to a man there."

"Did you?" Grammie asked pleasantly. "What about?"

"About going there to watch the moon-walk on their TV. He said I could. He said you could come, too. He made me promise you'd come. And Jenny. He said he'd fetch us in his car."

Grammie put her trowel into the basket. "Well, it will be a little late for me, I think. And for Jenny, too." She rose slowly and picked up her basket. "And very

late for you to go alone, don't *you* think?"

Adam was astounded. "You mean we can't go?" he cried in disbelief. "I can't go down there to see it? And you don't *want* to see it, and Jenny isn't going to . . ." And so on and so on.

Grammie waited until he stopped. Then she sighed and put her basket down again. She looked seriously at him. "I'm sorry, Adam," she said. "I see I've been quite thoughtless about this whole thing. I am only just beginning to understand what it means to you. Of course you may go if they will fetch you and bring you back. But you must excuse me; I will under no circumstances go with you. And Jenny will stay home with me."

"But why?" Adam questioned hotly. "They want you to come, too. Even more than me."

Grammie smiled slightly, nodding her head. "I'm sure they do."

Adam was bewildered. "Then why won't you come? Why? You have to tell me!"

"Very well," Grammie said, nodding again. "Perhaps I do, since it is so important to you. But you will probably not agree with me or my reasons." She looked down into the valley in the direction of the white house. "It is simply that I am not a friend of theirs. Last year they tried to keep your grandpa and me from buying that piece of land up there behind the house."

She waved her arm toward it, and Adam looked up at the crest of the mountain. Thick with stately pines, it lay hushed in the heat of the day. "We'd already put a down payment on it," Grammie continued. "Grandpa had always said we should own it, for our own protection, but we couldn't afford to buy it before then. Well, they tried to stop us, through the bank and with their lawyers and so on. They wanted to buy it themselves to put another ski lift on. But they didn't succeed. Of course, now that I am alone, they think everything may change. They think I may decide to sell the land, the farm and all, and move away. So they will do anything to get back in my good graces."

Adam was shocked. So that was why they had been so friendly. That was why they had wanted to know his name. They weren't interested in the moon-walk at all, just in ski lifts and—what had Grammie said?—"beer halls and hot-dog stands." Well, he didn't care. He would go anyway. What did it have to do with him? He looked up at the farmhouse. Jenny was calling to them from her window.

"I'm coming," Grammie called back. She gave Adam a friendly pat on his head as she left. Adam returned to his digging. Then he stopped again. An earthworm was slowly pushing through the clods of earth on the pitchfork. Adam put the pitchfork down and, crouching, watched the worm's gradual progress. "They breathe through the skin," he remembered from his science class. And what else? Yes, earthworms were good for the soil. They made it more fertile for growing things. What if he had hurt it with the pitchfork? He looked closely at the worm. It seemed to be all right. Then he picked it up. He had never touched a worm before, but somehow he was not frightened of it. It lay, cool and moist, on his palm. Then he remembered that earthworms did not like being out in the dry, warm air. He put it down on a patch of garden where he had already finished digging. Bit by bit, the worm burrowed itself into the loose soil.

But what would happen to it, Adam wondered, if Grammie's garden was no longer there, suddenly made into a parking lot or something? (All those skiers would need some place for their cars.) For that matter, what would happen to *everything?* Adam looked around him at the peaceful slopes. He listened to the sounds: the sighing rustle of leaves on the maple trees near the house, the occasional chirrup of a katydid, a cardinal calling tew-wee tew-wee tew-wee tew from the tall top of a pine by the road. But mostly, it was as though he were listening to a motionless silence, a hush that lay over him and the house and the road and the meadows and the evergreen mountains. Through that hush, he could hear the swift passage of the brook from the valley far below.

Well, there would still be cardinals, and the brook. They'd probably have to cut down an awful lot of those big trees, though, and build stuff: restaurants and a place to rent skis and boots and the parking lot. Motels, too, maybe. Anyway, more than just hot-dog stands and beer halls! Much more.

Adam frowned under the hot sun. He had done enough digging for now. Bending down, he looked for his worm, but it had gone, deep into the soil of Grammie's garden. Adam thought about Grammie and her garden. If she were planting things, didn't that mean she would *stay* on the farm? Surely she wouldn't be planting them for someone else to harvest. But maybe she *would* be too lonely here, all by herself. But *was* it lonely, with so many living and growing things everywhere you looked? Adam picked up the pitchfork and stepped carefully out of the garden, over the newly turned earth. He must remember to ask Grammie what she was going to do.

Friday evening

Downstairs in the living room after supper, Jenny was laughing. It was a gurgly sort of chuckling sound. Adam used to think it was cute and had loved to tickle her just to hear it. Now, up in his room, Adam heard it with annoyance. A thunderstorm was on its way, and the radio was full of static. But he had heard enough to tell him that he had missed a really good TV transmission from space. Mission Control called it a "superb" quality picture. It had been seen "live" in the United States, Japan, Western Europe, and South America. But not there in Grammie's house. Oh no, in Grammie's house there were "so many other things to do," who needed television?

When the astronauts retired for the night, sixty hours into the mission, Adam went to bed, too. It was still early, but the sky was dark with thunderclouds and the radio emitted only a shrill, crackling sound.

Saturday morning

After breakfast, Adam spent a long time transferring information from the newspaper to his charts. Jenny was out in the meadows and brought a caterpillar and a cricket home to lunch. She fed them some lettuce and let them go again. Before her nap she went with Grammie to the pasture to visit Lisa. Adam stayed by the radio as the spacecraft was due to go into orbit around the moon. It was a critical stage. When finally it was announced that Apollo 11 had come "around the corner" of the moon in the correct orbit, Adam was elated. "Whoopee!" he shouted from his window, and "Whoopee!" the sound came back, but whether it was Jenny answering or an echo from the surrounding mountains, he could not tell.

Saturday evening

In his room Adam was drawing a picture of an astronaut in a lunar space suit. It was a very careful and detailed drawing. It even showed the pocket for the penlight on the space suit sleeve. The valley lay in stillness except for the singing of the crickets and the frogs. Jenny had gone to bed.

"Adam?" It was Grammie knocking softly at his door. She came in and sat on his bed. Adam's many newspaper clippings lay scattered around her on the quilt.

"I don't like to interrupt," she began, "but something has happened, Adam, and I need your help."

It was poor old Lisa. She was not well. Grammie had noticed it the minute she and Jenny had gone into the pasture that afternoon. A fever perhaps and a bad leg and difficulty in breathing. And Grammie had seen those things before in other old animals about to die.

"She will be very bad by tomorrow," Grammie said sadly. "I have called the vet, and he will come early in the morning with a truck. He will take Lisa away, before

Jenny is awake, I hope. But this is the thing, Adam. I would like to go with them. That means I must ask you for your help with Jenny until I come back."

Adam felt chilled at the back of his neck. Lisa, going away to die? And Jenny! How would she ever understand that?

"I will tell her," Grammie said. "But not tomorrow. If she asks you, tell her that Lisa has probably wandered off somewhere and I will find her when I get back. She often used to do that," she recalled fondly. Then she got up and looked over Adam's head at the table, leaning her hands lightly on his shoulders. "What a nice drawing!" she exclaimed, seeing the astronaut. Adam looked miserably at it.

"What shall I do with Jenny while you're gone?"

Grammie pursed her lips and stood thinking for a minute. "Could you take her down to the brook? I'll leave you some sandwiches, and you could have a picnic lunch there. Later you could bring her up for her nap, and I would be back by the time she wakes up. And then you would be free to listen to the radio reports in the afternoon."

Adam nodded. He could do that, he guessed. Grammie thanked him and started toward the door.

"Grammie?" Adam said then.

"Yes?"

"*Are* you going to sell the farm? I mean, maybe you *are* going to move away or something."

"Should I?" Grammie said, giving him a keen look. "Would you?"

Adam remembered again the feel of the earthworm on his palm. He heard again the calm hush over everything. What had there been in yesterday's sun-warmed afternoon that he had not met before? He was not sure, but when he shook his head, it was a firm enough shake. "No," he replied finally. "I wouldn't."

Grammie nodded. "Neither would I. I'm staying right here." She went out, shutting the door quietly so as not to wake Jenny.

Adam picked up his pencil again. There didn't seem to be anything more to do on the astronaut. He took another sheet of paper and drew Lisa's eye as he remembered it: big and gentle, with eyelashes all around.

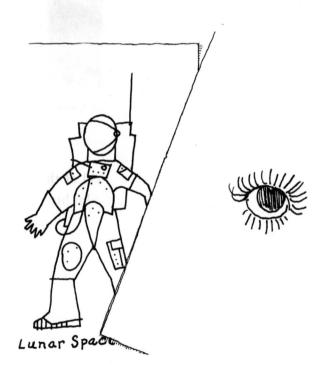

Lunar Space

Sunday morning

From the bridge Adam and Jenny followed the brook upward, away from the big pool and the house. Under the covering trees the air was cool and the light was dappled.

The brook had a pebbly edge they could walk along. In places where there was no edge, they jumped from stone to stone. Adam, carrying the bag with the picnic lunch, got his sneakers wet right away. Jenny jumped like a frog, her skinny legs flashing out and under, never missing. The water curled between the rocks. Rippling swiftly along, it carried now a brown leaf, now a twig, now a feather. The pools it made were clear as glass. Tiny minnows sparkled along the pebbled lining of the bottom. On each side, up steep, leafy banks, there were scurryings in the bushes. Woodchucks and badgers, Adam thought, wondering how he could know that. Presently they came to a bend in the brook. The water swirled prettily around the edges of the rocks. Jenny wanted to build a dam there. Soon, by moving shiny stones from one place to another, they had made a quiet lakelet next to the wide rock Jenny crouched on.

"Now make a boat, Adam. Make me a boat!" Jenny

was happy. She took off her sneakers and socks and climbed down into the middle of her shallow pool. "Ooooh," she squealed, climbing out again, "it's freeeeeeezing!"

Adam found the right-sized leaf and carefully stuck a thin twig through it. A second leaf made a sail. He launched the completed boat from his side of Jenny's pool, and it skimmed over the water to her.

"Let me! Let me!" Jenny cried in delight, scooping it up. Adam made several more boats for her. Then, growing tired of it, he stood up and looked around.

Something caused him to walk a bit farther upstream. He could still see Jenny; it was not far. But there, farther along the dwindling brook, he found his own pool. There was the very pool he himself had built seven years before. He remembered it perfectly: its shape, its stones, its dappled surface. And for a complete moment, he remembered his grandfather, too. He could quite clearly hear Grandpa saying, "You know, those woods are full of badgers and woodchucks," and his rolling voice reciting:

> "Dark brown is the river,
>   Golden is the sand;
>   It flows along forever,
>   With trees on either hand. . . ."

Adam looked into the pool at his reflected head and the shimmering leaves behind.

"Dark brown is the river," he said aloud. It was true. And it did flow along forever, year after year. Now Grandpa was gone. And now there was Jenny, building pools.

"Adam!" Jenny called just then. "I'm very, very, very hungry. Can't we have the picnic?"

Yes, the picnic. And afterward he would say for her the poem Grandpa had said for him. She was sure to like that.

Suddenly he realized they would have to hurry. It was almost time for the lunar module "Eagle" to separate from the command module "Columbia." He had to be near the radio then. He wasn't going to miss that for any little sister and a sick horse, no matter what.

Sunday afternoon

Adam filled in his charts as he listened to the radio. "GET (Ground Elapsed Time) 100:14, undocking safely completed," he wrote carefully, not letting his handwriting show how shaky with relief he was. He almost felt like adding, "Jenny safely in bed for nap," but decided it would not be very scientific. Aside from insisting on a visit to her "radish babies" when they had reached the farm, Jenny had been no trouble so far. It was even cute to see her dig in the earth around the radishes and then carefully cover them up again for their naps.

Adam listened with one ear to the radio and with the other for the sound of Grammie's taxi coming up the dirt road. But the time passed, and she did not come. That was annoying as Jenny would be waking soon and he didn't want her to bother him now—not now when the lunar module was just about to begin its descent to the surface of the moon. He had no time for Jenny now.

But Grammie did not come, and sure enough when, behind the moon, the astronauts were starting up the descent engine, Jenny appeared in the door of Adam's room. She stood there looking sleepy-eyed and damp-haired and asking him to put her sneakers on for her.

"Why can't you do that yourself?" Adam exclaimed.

"I can," Jenny confessed. "But I want you to do it."

Adam glanced out of the window in desperation. Where *was* Grammie? He tied Jenny's laces with a few fierce motions.

"Now sit down somewhere and keep still," he told her. "I'm listening to the radio, and I can't hear if you talk."

"I'm going out to see my radish babies," Jenny stated. Adam knew he could see the garden from his window, so that would be all right.

"OK," he agreed. "But stay where I can see you."

Little by little the voices on the radio became crisp with tension. In between progress reports from Houston, Adam took quick looks at Jenny in the garden and listened for Grammie's taxi.

Then came the long-awaited moment. Mission Control said, "Eagle, if you read, you're go for powered descent."

And at the same moment Adam realized that Jenny was gone! The garden was empty!

"Jenny!" Adam called. There was no answer. How long had she been gone? He wasn't sure. He checked his charts. The lunar module was due to touch down on the moon in fifteen minutes! Jenny would have to wait. He couldn't leave to look for her now. She would be all right, he told himself.

From the control center and from thousands of miles out in space came the voices:

CONTROL: "Altitude now 21,000 feet. Still looking very good. Velocity down now to 1,200 feet per second."

HOUSTON: "Eagle, you're looking great, coming up . . . nine minutes."

CONTROL: "We're now in the approach phase . . . looking good. Altitude 5,200 feet."

HOUSTON: ". . . you're go for landing, over."

EAGLE: "Roger, understand, go for landing . . . we're go, hang tight . . ."

And then, from somewhere outside, Adam realized Jenny was calling him. He could hear her run noisily into the house and come clattering up the stairs.

"Adam, Adam!" she was calling. "I can't find Lisa! I went to her field and she's not there! She's not anywhere! I called and called!"

Adam swung around in his chair. "Shut up for a minute!" he exclaimed irritably, waving her away. "I can't hear, and they're just landing now!"

But Jenny came and tugged at his arm. Adam pushed her away, trying to hear the radio.

EAGLE: "Got the shadow out there . . . 3½ down, 220 feet . . . 13 forward . . . 11 forward, coming down nicely . . . 75 feet, things looking good."

They were almost down. Adam stared, breathless, at the brown wood of the radio. Jenny pulled him again, crying, "Where is she? Where's Lisa? And where's Grammie?" Her voice was shrill with dismay.

Adam pressed his ear against the radio and turned up the volume.

EAGLE: "Lights on . . . down 2½ . . . forward . . . forward . . . good . . . 40 feet, down 2½ . . . picking up some dust."

JENNY (*who was shouting*): "Lisa! I can't find Lisa! Come and help me!"

ADAM (*hissing*): "Shut up! Shut up! They're landing! Right now! They're landing on the moon!"

JENNY (*shrill-voiced*):"I don't care about the moon! I want Lisa! Where is she?!"

ADAM (*furiously*): "Who cares about Lisa! Anyway, she's *gone,* that's what!"

JENNY (*howling*): *"Where?! Where's she gone?"*

ADAM (*bellowing now*): "I don't *know* where! And I CAN'T HEAR! (*Then suddenly, quiet and menacing*) Yes, I *do* know. I know exactly where she's gone. And I know she's never coming back because she's dead. Lisa's *dead!* (*Then, shouting again*) And now that you know, GET OUT OF HERE! *GET OUT AND STAY OUT!"*

He saw Jenny's white face staring at him, open-mouthed. He heard her gasp, and in the silence he heard the radio.

EAGLE: "Tranquility Base here. The Eagle has landed."

Jenny turned and ran from the room.

Sunday evening

There were no more voices now. Adam crouched on the ground in the vegetable garden, where Jenny had run, and held her in his arms. Her tears had wet straight through his shirt. She had finally stopped

crying, but Adam did not know how long they had been out there.

He looked down at Jenny's tangled hair in horror. He had no idea how to repair what he had done. He could only hold her as he had seen their mother do—as Grammie would have done. But he did not know what to say.

Inside the house, the telephone rang. Adam pried himself loose from Jenny and ran in to answer it. It was Grammie.

She was terribly sorry. She had been delayed . . . not one taxi driver was willing to take anyone anywhere . . . they were all glued to their television sets . . . impossible to get through earlier by telephone . . . even the operators wouldn't answer. Had he heard the landing?

"Yes," Adam said, in a dull voice. "I heard it."

"And Jenny? Is she all right?" Grammie asked, sensing something.

He told her what had happened. She was silent for a few seconds on the other end of the line.

"All right, Adam, don't worry," she said finally. "It couldn't be helped. See if you can take her mind off it until I get back. I should be there in about an hour. It's the best I can do. Could you get your own suppers? There's some left-over chicken in the icebox. And plenty of cookies and things." They would manage, Adam said.

Before returning to Jenny, Adam ran up to his room. The radio was still on. He knew the astronauts were scheduled to eat their first lunar meal, then to rest for four hours before preparing to leave the module. To his great surprise there was a change in the plan. The radio announced that the moon-walk would be four hours earlier than scheduled. No wonder! Who could rest peacefully with the moon waiting to be explored outside the door? He began to make alterations on his charts.

"Jenny," he reminded himself out loud. What was the matter with him? He turned off the radio and ran downstairs.

She was still lying in the garden, in the radish patch, crushing green leaves.

"You're lying on your radish babies," Adam told her. She moved a little and lifted a very tear- and dirt-stained face to see what damage she had done. Adam helped her to get up. "Come inside, Jenny. It's almost time for supper. Grammie will be here soon, right after we eat."

Jenny allowed herself to be steered toward the house. "I'm not hungry." She sniffled.

But the cats were. They were waiting in a crowd on the porch. Jenny stooped down and buried her face in the orange fur of one of them. "Can I feed them?"

Could she! Adam was more than happy to let her. The cats ate greedily, but Jenny and Adam only nibbled at their own food. Adam had many things on his mind. The moon-walk—would the men down by the brook know about the time change? Should he telephone them to tell them? How could he find out their telephone number when he didn't know their names?

What if Grammie didn't come back in time for him to go down there?

But it was hard to concentrate on all those questions. It was much easier to see that Jenny needed to be tidied up before Grammie *did* come back. She would have a dreadful fright seeing Jenny the way she looked now.

Just then the telephone rang again. He knew who it was before he answered it.

"This is your friendly neighbor," a man's voice said cheerfully. Did Adam know about the time change? When would his grandmother like them to come with the car? Could they have a word with her?

"No," Adam replied briefly, knowing that Grammie certainly wouldn't want to do that. "She's not here. And she's not going to watch the moon-walk anyway."

"Oh?" said the voice on the other end, after a very definite pause. "Why not?"

"As if you didn't know," Adam thought. But what should he tell them? Could he say, "She doesn't like you," or, "She knows you're after her land?" He didn't dare. But he had to say something. So he opened his mouth and said the first thing that came into his head. He couldn't have surprised himself more when he heard it.

"She just doesn't feel like it," he said clearly. "And

as a matter of fact, neither do I, anymore. Thank you very much, but I've changed my mind. I won't be coming after all." *Had* he changed his mind? When? He didn't know. It had happened without even thinking about it. He only knew that going down to the house by the brook would be going to the wrong place at the wrong time. He said good-bye and hung up the receiver.

"Who was that?" Jenny asked when he returned to the kitchen. Adam told her. "What did they want?" she persisted.

"They wanted to know if we are coming to watch television at their house tonight. To see the astronauts walk on the moon."

"Oh," said Jenny. "Are we?"

"No," Adam said. "We're going to hear it on the radio. And come on, you better get washed before Grammie comes home. You're a mess."

In the bathroom Jenny looked at her face in the mirror. First she thought it looked funny. Then she remembered why it looked that way. Adam saw tears begin to well up in her eyes.

"I won't ever see Lisa anymore," she said, half to herself. Adam felt a wave of panic.

"No, you won't," he agreed. "But there are other things. There are the cats. And your radish babies.

And caterpillars and things." He groped in his mind for something else to tell her. "And Lisa was old— very old and sick."

"Is that why she had to die?"

"I think so," said Adam. "Yes, so it's really better for her."

"Like it was better for Grandpa?"

"Did Grammie tell you that?" Jenny nodded. "Then, yes, like that," Adam agreed. He scrubbed at Jenny's face and hands with her washcloth, noticing for the first time in a long while how tiny everything about her was: her nose, her fingers, her thin wrists.

Finally she was in bed, with the light on, waiting for Grammie to come home. Her panda bear and three of the cats were nestled here and there on the quilt. She had put her nightgown on by herself, and it had ended up back to front.

On the moon the astronauts were putting on their moon suits: the same fiber glass, nylon-plastic, double-layered thermal meteoroid garments, equipped with sockets for oxygen and water tubes and containing an incredibly complex communication system, that Adam had drawn the night before. All over the world, people gaped at their television screens, waiting to see the first human being step onto the moon.

"If you want me, I'll be in my room, listening to the radio," Adam told Jenny at her door.

She looked up at him solemnly. "Are they really going to walk on the moon tonight?" she asked.

"Yes," Adam said.

"That's going to feel funny," Jenny reflected.

"Why?" Adam asked.

"Because the moon is made of green cheese—that's why."

Adam stared at her. She was as solemn as ever. Had Grammie told her that? He didn't know whether to laugh or scold. Instead, he did neither, but nodded thoughtfully. "Yes," he said. "I forgot. That sure will feel funny." He went out, leaving her door open so she could call him if she wanted.

Just then they heard the sound of Grammie's taxi coming up the road to the house.